LITTLE CRITTER®'S
PICTURE
DICTIONARY

 Children's Publishing

Columbus, Ohio

Credits:
McGraw-Hill Children's Publishing Editorial/Production Team
Vincent F. Douglas, B.S. and M. Ed.
Tracey E. Dils
Andrea Pelleschi
Teresa A. Domnauer
Lindsay Mizer

Big Tuna Trading Company Art/Editorial/Production Team
Mercer Mayer
John R. Sansevere
Erica Farber
Brian MacMullen
Matthew Rossetti
Kamoon Song
Soojung Yoo

 **Children's Publishing**

Send all inquiries to: McGraw-Hill Children's Publishing, 8787 Orion Place, Columbus OH 43240-4027

1-57768-839-2 (PB), 1-57768-380-3 (HC)

1 2 3 4 5 6 7 8 9 10 PHXBK 09 08 07 06 05 04 03

Table of Contents

WELCOME TO CRITTERVILLE!

Spider

Frog

Grasshopper

Little Critter

Mouse

Little Sister

Dad

Kitty

Mom

Blue

Gator

Bat Child

Gabby

Bun Bun

Tiger

Maurice

Molly

Malcolm

4

A NOTE TO PARENTS

Congratulations on selecting the best in educational materials for your child from McGraw-Hill Children's Publishing, the nation's premier educational publisher. This picture dictionary features Mercer Mayer's Little Critter® and is designed especially for children ages 4 to 7. It is an early literacy tool for exploring and enhancing vital language skills, including reading and writing, as well as listening and speaking. The entry words in this book were carefully chosen from age-appropriate vocabulary lists and include sight words and high-frequency words. Learning first words is lots of fun with the help of Little Critter and his friends!

Not only can young children use the dictionary to make the connection between the written word and its meaning, older children can use it as a handy reference guide. An example sentence and a charming Little Critter picture accompany each word.

You can use this picture dictionary as a means to nurture a love for reading in your child. Here are some suggestions to get you started:

- Introduce your child to the lovable Critterville characters on page 4.
- Review the letters of the alphabet with your child using the alphabet chart on page 8. Talk about the sound or sounds that each letter makes.
- Show your child one of the entry words. The word listed appears in red type in the sentence. The illustrations give your child clues as he or she learns to identify and sound out words.
- Encourage your child to look through the dictionary and point to words and/or pictures that interest him or her. Have your child read the word (or say the name of the picture) aloud. Then, read the accompanying sentence to your child. Invite your child to point to the word in the sentence. Allow your child to read the sentence back to you.
- Explain to your child that the words in a dictionary are always in ABC order. Suggest to your child that he or she look up some example words such as cat, dog, mouse, or zoo. Show your child how to use the color index tabs along the sides of the pages as a guide.

As always, continue to nurture and encourage your child as he or she learns to read.

Sincerely,
McGraw-Hill Children's Publishing

How to Use Your Picture Dictionary

Your new picture dictionary is a book of words with accompanying pictures of Little Critter and his friends. Example sentences help define each word, and activity pages reinforce learning.

Use your picture dictionary to:
- Learn to read new words
- Learn to spell words correctly
- Learn how to put words in ABC order
- Learn what words mean

Here is an example of what you will see on the pages:

cat

Kitty is our cat.

Each word has a picture and a sentence below it. The word is in red in the sentence. When you are looking for a word, the picture can also help you find it.

butterfly, butterflies

The butterfly has colorful wings.

Some words have an irregular spelling to make them plural or to show another form of an action word. These are next to the regular form of the word.

The words in this picture dictionary are listed in ABC order, just like the alphabet.

A B C D E F G H I J K L M N O P Q R S T U V W X Y Z
a b c d e f g h i j k l m n o p q r s t u v w x y z

There are tabs with letters on the sides of the pages. These tabs show you where you are in the alphabet.

When you want to look up a word, say the word aloud and listen for the beginning sound. The first letter in the word tells you where to begin looking in the dictionary. You can find a word even if you are not sure how to spell it. For example, if you were looking up the word dog, you would go to the letter d. If you were looking up the word tree, you would go to the letter t.

Use the activity pages throughout the book and at the end of the book to practice the new words that you have learned.

My ABC's

Aa	Bb	Cc	
Dd	Ee	Ff	
Gg	Hh	Ii	
Jj	Kk	Ll	
Mm	Nn	Oo	
Pp	Qq	Rr	
Ss	Tt	Uu	
Vv	Ww	Xx	
Yy	Zz		

Aa

a, an

I have an apple and a banana.

about

I like to read books about animals.

above

The nest is above my head.

across

Tiger's house is across the street.

add

1 + 1 = 2
2 + 2 = 4
3 + 3 = 6
4 + 4 = 8

Miss Kitty teaches us to add.

address

My address is 1 Critter Lane.

afraid 무섭다
우려운, 무서운

리틀 크리터가 무서워한 어두운곳을

Little Critter is afraid of the dark.

after 우섰다
∧ 후에
∧ 다음에

나는

I put on my shoes after my socks.

afternoon 오후

나는 노아형에와 오후에

I play with Tiger in the afternoon.

10   오후에

again 또 다시 해다

정말 재미있는게임이야 또 게임

What a fun game. Let's play again! 핫자

air 공기, 공중.

저 새 좀 보세요 하늘을 날겠어요!

Look at the bird in the air!

airplane 비행기
공중에

여기오고있다 비행기가.

Here comes an airplane.

airport 공항

비행기가 안드어있는 공항으로

The airplane lands at the airport.

all

맥컴은 먹었다 그의 저녁식
모두의   사를

Malcolm ate all of his dinner.

almost

Our snowman is almost finished.

alone

Blue does not like to be alone.

already

리틀씨 벌써 먹었다
벌써   먹었다

Little Sister has already eaten.

also

리틀 크리터우 좋아 했다 아이스크림을
개비도
Little Critter likes ice cream. Gabby
also likes ice cream.
역 좋아했다 아이스크림

am

나는 행복 하다.

I am happy!

3/1

alphabet

Little Sister knows the alphabet.

a
b
c
d
e
f
g
h
i
j
k
l
m
n
o
p
q
r
s
t
u
v
w
x
y
z

and 그리고

Little Critter has milk and cookies.
eats

angry 화난

Why is Tiger so angry?

animal 동물

Which animal is your favorite?
앝

answer 답

Gator knows the answer.

ant 개미

An ant has six legs.

any 어떤 약간의

Little Critter/doesn't have/any cookies.

ape 유인원

The ape /eats /a banana./

12

apple

There is / a worm / in Dad's apple.
읽다

are
am
is
① ~이다
② ~에 있다

Maurice and Molly are in a race.
경주하다.

arm

This is my arm.

around
주위에

There are / flowers / all around us.
있다

art
미술, 예술

We love art class.

artist
미술
예술가

I am a great artist.

a b c d e f g h i j k l m n o p q r s t u v w x y z

ask

I **ask** Miss Kitty **for** help.

at

Dad **is at** the store.

aunt

My **aunt** is my mom's sister.

automobile

The **automobile** is blue.

awake

Little Critter **is awake**.

away

Blue **runs away** from me.

14

Bb

baby, babies

아기

Mom holds the baby.

back

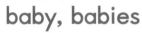

come back
다시

I have a bug on my back.

back

Blue is in back of the doghouse.

bad

나쁜

Sometimes Blue is bad.

bag

가방
봉지
자루

Bun Bun has a bag of candy.

bake

굽다

Mom can bake the best cookies.

15

ball

Throw the ball, Malcolm!

balloon

Little Sister has a blue balloon.

banana

Mom put a banana in my lunchbox.

band

I am the leader of the band.

bank

I put money in my bank.

barn

Grandpa paints the barn red.

baseball

We play baseball.

16

basket

바귀

Little Sister has a basket of flowers.

basketball

농구

Gator plays basketball.

bat

야구방망이

Tiger has the bat.

bath house

목욕

I give Blue a bath.

bathroom

화장실

The bathroom is a mess.

bathtub

목조

I take a bath in the bathtub.

beach, beaches

해변

Grandma and I play at the beach.

bear

The **bear** caught a fish.

beautiful

아름다운

Grandpa paints a **beautiful** picture.

bed

침대

The bed illustration with Little Sister.

Little Sister sleeps in her **bed**.

bee

벌

Dad sees the **bee**.

beep

경적을 울리다

BEEP!

Dad **beeps** his horn.

before

~ 전에

I put on my socks **before** my shoes.

18

begin

시작하다

The race is about to begin.

behind

뒤

Molly is behind the tree.

bell

종

Miss Kitty rings the bell after lunch.

below

아래

Gator is below Tiger.

bend

구부리다

I bend my arm.

beside

곁에

Little Sister stands beside the swing.

best

최고

This pie tastes the best.

better

더 좋은

I like ice cream better than carrots.

between

사이에

Mouse is between Kitty and Blue.

bicycle, bike

자전거

Tiger rides his bicycle to school.

big 크다

Gabby pets the big dog.

bird

새

The bird sits on the branch.

birthday

생일파티!

Today is my birthday!

bite

물다

Tiger takes a **bite** of his pizza.

black

검은색

The crow is **black**.

blocks

블럭

Bat Child plays with **blocks**.

blow

불다

Blow out the candles, Little Sister!

blue

파랑색

The whale is **blue**.

boat

보트

Malcolm rows the **boat**.

bone

뼈

Where did Blue put his **bone**?

book

책

Gabby reads her favorite book.

boot

부츠

I put on my boots to go outside.

both

둘 다

Both of us like cupcakes.

bottom

바닥

Mouse is at the bottom of the stairs.

bow

리본

Little Sister's bow has red polka dots.

bowl

공깨

Blue's bowl is empty.

box, boxes

상자

Blue hides in the box.

boy

Little Critter is a boy.

bread

I like peanut butter on my bread.

breakfast

I make breakfast for Little Sister.

bring

I bring Dad the newspaper.

broken

The vase is broken.

brother

Maurice is Molly's brother.

brown

The teddy bear is brown.

bubble

I blow a big bubble.

bug

Look at the funny bug!

bump

I bump into the table.

bump

I have a bump on my elbow.

bunny, bunnies

Bat Child has too many bunnies.

bus, buses

We ride the bus to school.

A
B
C
D
E
F
G
H
I
J
K
L
M
N
O
P
Q
R
S
T
U
V
W
X
Y
Z

butterfly, butterflies

The butterfly has colorful wings.

buy

Gabby wants to buy a lollipop.

button

Dad's shirt needs a new button!

by

Maurice is standing by Molly.

25

Aa Bb Activity Page

Word List

airplane	alligator	ant	ball
baseball	bear	blocks	

Read each word in the Word List. Then point to the object that goes with each word in the picture above.

Cc

cake

Gator baked a cake.

call

I call Grandpa.

camp

We go to camp in the summer.

can

I can write my name.

can

Do you want a can of soup?

candy, candies

Candy is sweet.

A
B
C
D
E
F
G
H
I
J
K
L
M
N
O
P
Q
R
S
T
U
V
W
X
Y
Z

a
b
c
d
e
f
g
h
i
j
k
l
m
n
o
p
q
r
s
t
u
v
w
x
y
z

cap

I have a red cap.

car

Dad drives our car.

care

I care for Mom when she is sick.

carrot

Bun Bun eats a carrot.

carry, carries

We carry wood for the fire.

cat

Kitty is our cat.

catch, catches

I can catch the ball.

chair

Mom sleeps in the chair.

cherry, cherries

Cherries are red and sweet.

chicken

The chicken sits on her eggs.

child, children

Mr. and Mrs. Critter have two children.

circle

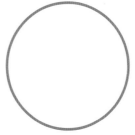

Can you draw a circle?

city, cities

My uncle lives in the city.

A
B
C
D
E
F
G
H
I
J
K
L
M
N
O
P
Q
R
S
T
U
V
W
X
Y
Z

a
b
c
d
e
f
g
h
i
j
k
l
m
n
o
p
q
r
s
t
u
v
w
x
y
z

clap

I clap my hands.

class, classes

I have friends in my class.

clay

I made a vase out of clay.

clean

I help clean up after dinner.

clock

A clock tells the time.

close

They sit close to stay warm.

close

Close the door, Tiger.

clothes

Little Sister put on her clothes.

cloud

That cloud is white.

coat

I wear my new purple coat.

cold

Mom has a bad cold.

cold

It is cold outside!

color

What is your favorite color?

a
b
c
d
e
f
g
h
i
j
k
l
m
n
o
p
q
r
s
t
u
v
w
x
y
z

come

Gabby can come to my party.

computer

Gabby works on the computer.

cook

Dad likes to cook outside.

cookie

I give Dad a cookie.

cool

The pool is cool on a hot day.

corn

Grandpa grows corn.

count

Little Sister can count to ten.

32

cow

Grandpa milks the cow.

crayon

I draw with a crayon.

cry, cries

The baby cries loudly.

cub

The mother bear is with her cub.

cup

I have a cup of hot cocoa.

cut

Little Critter cuts the paper.

cute

The little kitten is cute.

dad, daddy

My **dad** is very smart. I like to call him **Daddy**.

dance

Gabby likes to **dance**.

danger

The police officer keeps us from **danger**.

dark

Malcolm is afraid of the **dark**.

date

What is the **date** on the calendar?

daughter

Little Sister is Dad's **daughter**.

day

What a sunny **day** it is!

deep

The water looks **deep**.

deer

The **deer** has brown fur.

dentist

The **dentist** cleans my teeth.

desk

Little Critter sits at his **desk**.

different

I have two **different** mittens!

dig

My dog likes to **dig**.

a
b
c
d
e
f
g
h
i
j
k
l
m
n
o
p
q
r
s
t
u
v
w
x
y
z

dinner

We eat **dinner** with Grandma and Grandpa.

dinosaur

Tyrannosaurus Rex is a scary **dinosaur**.

dirt

The truck dumps the **dirt**.

dish, dishes

I clean the **dishes**.

do, does

Gator **does** his homework every night. **Do** you?

doctor

The **doctor** takes care of me.

36

dog

My **dog** is brown and white.

doll

Little Sister holds her **doll**.

down

We go **down** the slide.

draw

I can **draw** a dinosaur.

dream

Gator has a **dream** about sheep.

dress, dresses

Little Sister wears a pink **dress**.

drink

Tiger likes to drink milk.

drive

Dad will drive us to the library.

drop

Oops! Malcolm drops his ice cream.

dry, dries

I dry Blue after his bath.

dry

The clothes are dry.

duck

The duck has webbed feet.

Cc Dd Activity Page

	Word List		
cake	cat	chair	cookie
dish	doll	dress	duck

Read each word in the Word List. Then point to the object that goes with each word in the picture above.

39

a
b
c
d
e
f
g
h
i
j
k
l
m
n
o
p
q
r
s
t
u
v
w
x
y
z

E e

ear

Bun Bun can wiggle her **ear**.

easy

It is **easy** to stand on one leg.

early

I got up **early** this morning.

eat

Tiger and Gator **eat** peanuts.

Earth

We live on the planet **Earth**.

egg

Oops! I broke an **egg**.

eight, 8

A spider has **eight** legs.

elbow

I like to lean on my **elbow**.

elephant

The **elephant** has a long nose.

empty

The glass is **empty**!

end

Gabby is at the **end** of the line.

every

I brush my teeth **every** morning.

eyes

We see with our **eyes**.

Ff

face

I wash my face.

fall

We rake leaves in the fall.

fall

The apples fall from the tree.

family, families

This is Maurice and Molly's family.

far

Tiger hits the ball far.

farm

Grandma and Grandpa live on a farm.

farmer

Grandpa is a **farmer**.

fast

Our sled goes really **fast**!

fat

That is a **fat** cat!

father

I look like my **father**.

feed

I **feed** my dog every day.

feel

I **feel** happy today!

feeling

Mom is **feeling** sick today.

a
b
c
d
e
f
g
h
i
j
k
l
m
n
o
p
q
r
s
t
u
v
w
x
y
z

few

I only have a **few** crayons.

fight

Blue and Kitty **fight** over the ball.

fill

Dad **fills** the pool with water.

find

I **find** a snake under the rock.

finger

Bun Bun has a bug on her **finger**.

fire

We toast marshmallows over the **fire**.

fire fighter

The **fire fighter** let me wear his helmet.

44

first

Little Critter is **first** in line.

fish, fishes

Dad **fishes** every weekend. Today he caught a big **fish**!

fit

This hat does not **fit** me.

five, 5

There are **five** apples.

fix, fixes

Dad **fixes** the broken vase.

flag

Gator has a **flag**.

floor

I got mud on the floor.

flower

I grew the flower all by myself!

fly, flies

The bird flies away.

follow

Blue likes to follow me wherever I go.

food

Pizza is my favorite food.

foot, feet

I have 2 feet.

football

Maurice kicks the football.

fork

I need a fork to eat.

four, 4

Tiger juggles four balls.

friend

Tiger is a good friend.

frog

This is my frog.

front

Blue is in front of the doghouse.

fruit

There is fruit in the bowl.

full

The bag is **full** of food.

funny

Malcolm is **funny**.

fur

This dog has a lot of **fur**.

fun

Soccer is **fun** to play!

Ee Ff Activity Page

Read each word in the Word List. Then point to the object that goes with each word.

a
b
c
d
e
f
g
h
i
j
k
l
m
n
o
p
q
r
s
t
u
v
w
x
y
z

Gg

game

We play a game.

gift

Little Critter gives Little Sister a gift.

garden

I help Grandma water the garden.

giraffe

The giraffe has a long neck.

get

I get the mail for Mom.

girl

Little Sister is a girl.

give

I **give** Little Critter a valentine.

glad

Little Critter is **glad**.

glass, glasses

Little Critter has a **glass** of milk.

glasses

Grandpa needs **glasses** to read.

glue

The **glue** is very sticky.

go, goes

A green light means **go**.

goat

The **goat** eats grass.

goldfish

Tiger has a goldfish.

good

This ice cream tastes good!

good-bye

We say good-bye to Gabby.

good night

I say good night to Little Sister.

goose, geese

Two geese fly away. One goose does not.

grandfather, grandmother

My grandmother and grandfather live on a farm.

grapes

Gabby and I eat grapes.

grass

Dad cuts the grass in our yard.

grasshopper

The grasshopper has long legs.

great

Blue is a great dog.

green

The tree is green.

grow

I grow a little every year.

guitar

Bat Child plays the guitar.

gum

That gum is sticky!

a
b
c
d
e
f
g
 h
i
j
k
l
m
n
o
p
q
r
s
t
u
v
w
x
y
z

hair

The barber cuts my hair.

hamster

The hamster likes his ball.

hand

I have two pencils in my hand.

happy

Tiger is happy on his birthday.

hard

It is hard to climb a tree.

hard

The turtle's shell is very hard.

54

has

Molly has a new dress.

hat

I have a cowboy hat.

have

I also have a lasso.

hay

I feed hay to the cow.

he

Gator likes to draw. He is a good artist.

head

I hit the soccer ball with my head.

healthy

Dr. Horn helps me stay healthy.

e
f
g
h
i
j
k
l
m
n
o
p
q
r
s
t
u
v
w
x
y
z

Can you **hear** the music?

heart

I can draw a **heart**.

heavy

These weights are **heavy**!

hello, hi

Little Critter says **hello** to Gator.
Gator says, "Hi."

help

Malcolm fell! I will **help** him get up.

hen

Gabby has a pet **hen**.

her

Little Sister can see **her** shadow.

here

Let's hang the picture **here**.

hers

That horn is **hers**.

hide

Kitty likes to **hide** in the basket.

high

Our kites are **high** above us.

hill

Gator sleds down the **hill**.

him

Blue is hiding. Do you see **him**?

A
B
C
D
E
F
G
H
I
J
K
L
M
N
O
P
Q
R
S
T
U
V
W
X
Y
Z

his

Little Critter walks **his** dog.

hit

What **hit** my head?

hog

The **hog** is a really big pig.

hold

I **hold** Mom's hand.

hole

Blue digs a **hole**.

holiday

Thanksgiving is a **holiday**.

home

This is my home.

homework

Gator does homework after school.

hop

Who can hop higher?

hope

I hope it stops raining.

horse

The horse has a long tail.

hot

The soup is hot!

a
b
c
d
e
f
g
h
i
j
k
l
m
n
o
p
q
r
s
t
u
v
w
x
y
z

hour

There are sixty minutes in one hour.

house

The house has a red roof.

hug

I hug Blue.

hug

Mom gives me a big hug.

hurry, hurries

I hurry to catch the bus.

hurt

Malcolm hurt his foot.

60

Gg Hh Activity Page

hug

hat

goose

goat

goldfish

heart

game

house

Look at each picture in the column on the left. Then point to the word that matches the picture in the column on the right.

a
b
c
d
e
f
g
h
i
j
k
l
m
n
o
p
q
r
s
t
u
v
w
x
y
z

I

I like to go fishing.

ice cream

Gabby and I have ice cream.

in

Blue is in the doghouse.

inside

We stay inside when it rains.

is

Kitty is sleeping.

it

Miss Kitty has an apple. It is red.

62

Jj

jam

I like grape jam.

jar

There is a bug in the jar.

jeans

Dad got new blue jeans.

jet

The jet lands at the airport.

job

It is my job to sweep the floor.

a
b
c
d
e
f
g
h
i
j
k
l
m
n
o
p
q
r
s
t
u
v
w
x
y
z

joke

Bat Child tells a funny joke.

judge

Gator is the judge for the costume contest.

jug

The juice comes in a jug.

juice

I like my peanut butter sandwich with orange juice on top.

jump

I can jump rope.

Ii Jj Activity Page

Word List

ice	ice cream	jam
jar	jeans	juice

Read each word in the Word List. Then point to the object that goes with each word in the picture above.

keep

I **keep** my goldfish in a bowl.

key

This is the **key** to my house.

kick

Tiger does a karate **kick**.

king

The **king** wears a crown.

kiss, kisses

Little Sister gives her doll a **kiss**.

kitchen

We eat in the **kitchen**.

66

kite

Tiger flies his yellow kite.

kitten

The kitten is two months old.

knee

I hurt my knee.

knock

Did you hear the knock on the door?

know

I know how to read.

a
b
c
d
e
f
g
h
i
j
k
l
m
n
o
p
q
r
s
t
u
v
w
x
y
z

lake

We fish in the lake.

lamb

A lamb is a baby sheep.

lamp

The lamp is on the table.

land

We saw a plane land at the airport.

lap

Little Sister sits on Dad's lap.

large

Dad is large. I am small.

last

Tiger is last in line.

late

Little Critter is late for school!

laugh

Bat Child likes to laugh.

leaf, leaves

The leaf is green.

learn

We learn math at school.

leave

We leave the clubhouse.

left

Little Critter writes with his left hand.

leg

Gator has a broken leg.

lemonade

Do you want some lemonade?

lend

I lend my mitt to Tiger.

let

Mom let us have some cookies.

letter

Gabby writes a letter.

letter carrier

The letter carrier brings the mail.

library, libraries

We read a book at the library.

light

The lamp gives us light.

like

I like spaghetti and meatballs.

line

We walk in a line.

A
B
C
D
E
F
G
H
I
J
K
L
M
N
O
P
Q
R
S
T
U
V
W
X
Y
Z

a
b
c
d
e
f
g
h
i
j
k

l
m
n
o
p
q
r
s
t
u
v
w
x
y
z

lion

The lion is big and strong.

listen

I listen to music.

little

Malcolm is big. Mouse is little.

live

I live in Critterville.

lizard

The lizard has a long tail.

log

The butterfly sits on the log.

long

The red pencil is long. The yellow pencil is short.

72

look

We look for treasure!

lose

I don't like to lose.

lot

Little Critter has a lot of books.

loud

The radio is very loud!

love

I love my dog.

low

The blue bird flies high. The red bird flies low.

lunch, lunches

Maurice and Molly eat lunch.

Kk Ll Activity Page

Word List

key	king	kite	kitten
lamp	lemonade	lion	log

Read each word in the Word List. Then point to the object that goes with each word.

74

A
B
C
D
E
F
G
H
I
J
K
L
M
N
O
P
Q
R
S
T
U
V
W
X
Y
Z

mad

I get mad when I lose things.

mailbox, mailboxes

Gabby puts a letter in the mailbox.

make

Mom is going to make a cake.

man, men

That man has red hair.

many

I have many pets.

mask

Bat Child wears a mask.

a
b
c
d
e
f
g
h
i
j
k
l
(m)
n
o
p
q
r
s
t
u
v
w
x
y
z

mat

I stand on the mat.

may

May I have this robot, please?

me

This is a picture of me!

mean

That angry dog looks mean!

measure

I measure the plants to see how much they grow.

meat

Malcolm has meat for dinner.

meet

Tiger and Gabby meet me under the tree.

mess

This is a big **mess**!

milk

It is good to drink **milk** every day.

mine

This kite is **mine**.

miss, misses

I **miss** Grandma and Grandpa.

mittens

I wear **mittens** when it snows.

mom, mommy

My **mom** reads to me. It is a story about a baby bear and its **mommy**.

money

Look at all the **money**.

monkey

The monkey plays with the ball.

monster

Look at the scary monster on TV!

moon

The moon is out tonight.

more

Bat Child has more balloons than Tiger.

morning

I get out of bed in the morning.

mother

I go shopping with my mother.

mountain

There is snow on top of the mountain.

mouse

The **mouse** has whiskers.

mice

The **mice** like to run together.

mouth

Little Sister looks in my **mouth**.

move

I can **move** this giant snowball.

mud

The pig plays in the **mud**.

music

The band plays lots of **music**.

my

This is **my** lunchbox.

a b c d e f g h i j k l m n o p q r s t u v w x y z

name

My **name** is Gator.

nap

Blue takes a **nap**.

near

The squirrel is **near** the tree.

new

Dad made a **new** birdhouse.

next

Bat Child is **next** in line.

nice

Miss Kitty is a **nice** teacher.

night

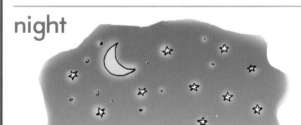

The moon and stars come out at **night**.

nine, 9

Gabby sees nine butterflies.

no

No, thank you.

nose

I smell with my nose.

now

Now it is time to sleep.

number

I can count to the number ten.

nurse

Molly wants to be a nurse.

nut

The squirrel eats a nut.

A
B
C
D
E
F
G
H
I
J
K
L
M
N
O
P
Q
R
S
T
U
V
W
X
Y
Z

Mm Nn Activity Page

Read each word in the Word List. Then point to the object that goes with each word.

oak

There is an oak tree in our yard.

ocean

Grandma and I play in the ocean.

octopus

An octopus has eight legs.

off

Little Critter is off the mat.

often

Little Sister often reads her favorite book before bed.

old

What will I look like when I'm old?

a
b
c
d
e
f
g
h
i
j
k
l
m
n
o
p
q
r
s
t
u
v
w
x
y
z

on

Bun Bun is **on** the swing.

one, 1

There is **one** apple.

only

Little Sister has **only** one lollipop.

open

The door is **open**.

or

Little Critter will eat either a hamburger **or** a hot dog.

orange

The **orange** is round and sweet.

orange

The carrot is bright **orange**.

our

This is our grandpa.

out

Little Sister takes the drum out of the box.

outside

It is raining outside.

oven

Grandma puts the pie in the oven.

over

Gabby is over Little Critter.

owl

The owl sits on a branch.

own

Little Sister has her own tricycle.

A
B
C
D
E
F
G
H
I
J
K
L
M
N
O
P
Q
R
S
T
U
V
W
X
Y
Z

P p

pad

I write on my pad.

pal

Tiger is my pal.

pan

Mom cooks eggs in a pan.

pants

Malcolm has new green pants.

paper

I will cut the paper.

park

We go to the park after school.

party, parties

We have a birthday party for Little Sister.

pass, passes

Pass the ball, Tiger!

pat

I pat the baby goat.

pay

GOOD STUFF!
COOKIES-
6 FOR $1.00
PIES
$2.00 A SLICE
$12.00 WHOLE

I pay Little Critter for the cupcake.

pen

Dad writes with a pen.

pencil

I do my homework with a pencil.

people

There are many different kinds of people.

pet

I pet the cat.

pet

Little Critter has a dog for a pet.

pickle

I put a pickle on my sandwich.

picture

This is a picture of my family.

pie

I am making a **pie**.

pig

The **pig** won first prize.

pin

Miss Kitty wears a pretty **pin**.

pizza

I eat **pizza** with my friends.

plant

I help Grandpa **plant** the tree.

plant

Mom has a new **plant**.

plate

Gabby put the **plate** on the table.

A
B
C
D
E
F
G
H
I
J
K
L
M
N
O
P
Q
R
S
T
U
V
W
X
Y
Z

play

We play with our toys.

playground

We have fun at the playground.

please

May I please come in?

pole

The birdhouse is on top of the pole.

police officer

The police officer says, "Stop!"

pony, ponies

A pony is a small horse.

pool

Bat Child gets in the **pool**.

pop

The balloon goes "**Pop!**"

popcorn

We love to eat **popcorn**.

pot

Be careful. The **pot** is hot!

present

I have a **present** for Little Sister.

pretty

The vase is filled with **pretty** flowers.

price

The doll only costs eight cents. That is a good price!

pull

I pull Gabby through the snow.

pumpkin

This is a perfect pumpkin.

puppy, puppies

Gator has a new puppy.

purple

Bun Bun wears purple overalls.

put

I put my clothes in the dresser.

92

Oo Pp Activity Page

Word List

octopus	open	orange	owl
pail	pencil	pig	pumpkin

Read each word in the Word List. Then point to the object that goes with each word.

quack

I hear the duck quack.

quick

The rabbit is quick!

queen

The queen wears a red robe.

quiet

Be quiet, Blue!

question

Raise your hand if you have a question.

quit

Even though he was losing, Little Critter did not quit the race.

Rr

rabbit

The **rabbit** has a fluffy tail.

radio

The **radio** plays music.

rain

When is the **rain** going to stop?

rake

Gator uses a **rake** to **rake** leaves.

rat

The **rat** likes cheese.

read

Mom likes to **read**.

A
B
C
D
E
F
G
H
I
J
K
L
M
N
O
P
Q
R
S
T
U
V
W
X
Y
Z

95

ready

We are **ready** for dinner.

red

The fire truck is bright **red**.

ride

Grandpa and I **ride** the horse.

right

Gabby writes with her **right** hand.

ring

Miss Kitty **rings** the bell.

ring

The **ring** is gold and shiny.

rip

My pocket has a **rip**.

river

The boat goes down the **river**.

road

The bus is on the **road**.

robin

The **robin** has a red breast.

robot

Look at my new toy **robot**.

rock

The spider crawls on the **rock**.

rocket

The **rocket** is ready for takeoff.

A
B
C
D
E
F
G
H
I
J
K
L
M
N
O
P
Q
R
S
T
U
V
W
X
Y
Z

room

I play in my **room**.

round

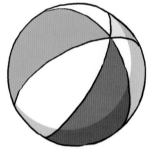

The ball is **round**.

row

I **row** my boat in the lake.

ruler

I use my **ruler** to measure.

rules

I follow the **rules** at the pool.

run

Little Sister can **run** around the track three times.

robin

rocket

queen

quack

ring

radio

rabbit

Look at each picture in the column on the left. Then point to the word that matches the picture in the column on the right.

a
b
c
d
e
f
g
h
i
j
k
l
m
n
o
p
q
r
(s)
t
u
v
w
x
y
z

S s

sad

Little Sister is sad.

safe

It is not safe to walk here.

same

We play on the same team.

sand

Little Sister plays in the sand.

sandwich, sandwiches

I have a sandwich for lunch.

say

ABCDEFGHIJKLM
NOPQRSTUVWXYZ!

Little Sister can say the alphabet.

100

school

We have a spelling bee at school.

sea

Some animals live in the sea.

seal

The seal has a ball.

second

Bat Child is second in line.

see

I see an elephant at the zoo.

seed

A seed will grow into a plant one day.

seesaw

The seesaw goes up and down.

sell

We **sell** lemonade.

send

I **send** a letter.

set

Grandma **set** the pan on the stove.

seven

There are **seven** seashells.

shake

Blue can **shake** my hand.

shape

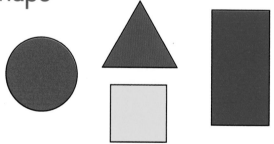

What is your favorite **shape**?

share

I **share** my lunch with Little Critter.

sharp

The shark has sharp teeth!

she

This is Little Sister. She likes waffles.

sheep

The sheep has fluffy white wool.

shirt

My favorite shirt is dirty.

shoe

Tiger found his shoe.

shop

We shop for fruit.

shop

This shop sells toys.

a
b
c
d
e
f
g
h
i
j
k
l
m
n
o
p
q
r
(s)
t
u
v
w
x
y
z

short

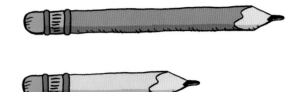

The red pencil is long. The yellow pencil is **short**.

shovel

I dig with a **shovel**.

shy

Bun Bun is **shy**.

sick

Tiger feels **sick**.

side

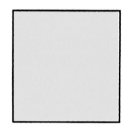

A square has four **sides**.

sing

Bun Bun and Little Sister **sing** together.

sister

I read to my **sister**.

sit

We **sit** on the swings.

six, 6

There are **six** little chicks.

skates

Look at my new **skates**.

skateboard

Tiger rides his **skateboard**.

skirt

Gabby wears a blue **skirt**.

skunk

The **skunk** is black and white.

A
B
C
D
E
F
G
H
I
J
K
L
M
N
O
P
Q
R
(S)
T
U
V
W
X
Y
Z

sky

There are clouds in the sky.

sleep

I sleep at night.

slow

The rabbit is fast. The turtle is slow.

small

The bug is small.

smart

Tiger knows the answer. He is smart.

smell

The flower has a pretty smell.

smile

I smile when I am happy.

smile

Malcolm has a big smile on his face.

snail

The snail carries his house on his back.

snake

Don't step on the snake!

snow

It's fun to play in the snow!

snowball

Gator throws a snowball.

snowman

We made a snowman.

a
b
c
d
e
f
g
h
i
j
k
l
m
n
o
p
q
r
s
t
u
v
w
x
y
z

soccer

Tiger plays **soccer**.

socks

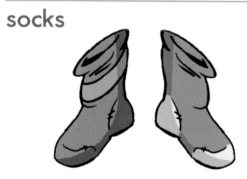

These **socks** don't match.

soft

The pillow is **soft**.

some

We eat **some** blueberries.

son

Little Critter is Mom's **son**.

song

Little Sister sings us a **song**.

soup

Little Critter eats alphabet **soup**.

spider

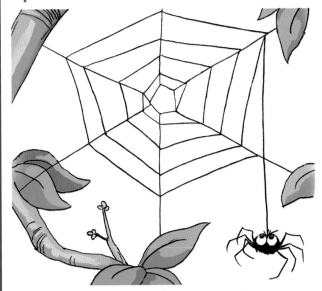

The spider hangs from a web.

spoon

Bat Child has a spoon.

sport

Football is Malcolm's best sport.

spring

Mom and I plant flowers in the spring.

squirrel

The squirrel has a bushy tail.

stand

I stand next to Gator.

A
B
C
D
E
F
G
H
I
J
K
L
M
N
O
P
Q
R
S
T
U
V
W
X
Y
Z

a
b
c
d
e
f
g
h
i
j
k
l
m
n
o
p
q
r
s
t
u
v
w
x
y
z

star

I see one bright star.

start

I am ready to start the day.

state

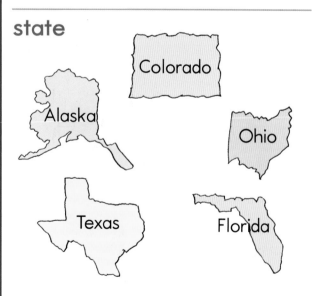

Which state do you live in?

stay

Blue does not stay in the yard.

stick

Little Critter throws a stick to Blue.

sticker

Miss Kitty put a star sticker on my paper.

sticky

The glue is very sticky!

stop

A red light means stop.

store

We buy paint and wood at the hardware store.

story, stories

I tell Bun Bun a story.

strawberry, strawberries

Strawberries are red and sweet.

street

Little Critter walks across the street.

string

I need string for my kite.

strong

Malcolm is strong.

A
B
C
D
E
F
G
H
I
J
K
L
M
N
O
P
Q
R
S
T
U
V
W
X
Y
Z

a
b
c
d
e
f
g
h
i
j
k
l
m
n
o
p
q
r
(s)
t
u
v
w
x
y
z

summer

We go to the beach in the summer.

sun

The sun is shining today.

surprise

My friends give me a surprise!

sweater

Mom bought Dad a new sweater.

sweet

The cotton candy tastes sweet!

swim

I like to swim.

table

My fish is on the table.

tag

Gator and I play tag with Gabby.

tail

The iguana has a long tail.

take

Malcolm takes some popcorn.

talk

I talk on the telephone.

tall

The mother giraffe is very tall.

taste

The chef **tastes** the soup.

teacher

Miss Kitty is my **teacher**.

telephone

There are twelve buttons on the **telephone**.

tell

I **tell** Bun Bun a secret.

ten, 10

There are **ten** gingerbread men.

tent

I help Dad set up the **tent**.

thank you

Thank **you** for the birthday present.

that

That is Grandpa's pig.

the

The sled goes fast.

their

Maurice and Molly eat their popcorn.

there

My school is over there.

they

Maurice and Molly are dressed as mittens. They are going to a party.

thing

What is that thing?

think

I think about my favorite things.

a
b
c
d
e
f
g
h
i
j
k
l
m
n
o
p
q
r
s
t
u
v
w
x
y
z

three, 3

There are **three** cupcakes.

throw

I **throw** the baseball.

thumb

I have a bandage on my **thumb**.

tie, ties

Tiger can **tie** his shoes.

tiger

The **tiger** has black stripes.

time

What **time** is it?

toad

A **toad** has bumps on his skin.

today

Today we are going to the zoo.

toe

I dip my toe in the water.

tonight

Dad and I are camping out tonight.

together

Maurice and Molly read together.

too

Little Critter has too many frogs!

tomorrow

Tomorrow is Monday.

tooth, teeth

My tooth came out!

a
b
c
d
e
f
g
h
i
j
k
l
m
n
o
p
q
r
s
t
u
v
w
x
y
z

toothpaste

Maurice brushes his teeth with toothpaste.

top

I put a cherry on top of my sundae.

town

Critterville is a small town.

toy

This robot is my favorite toy.

tractor

The farmer drives the tractor.

train

This robot is my favorite toy.

The train stops in Critterville.

tree

We play by the tree.

tricycle

A tricycle has three wheels.

truck

The truck is next to the tree.

try, tries

I try to run as fast as Tiger.

tummy

My tummy is full!

turkey

The turkey has many feathers.

turtle

The turtle has a shell.

two, 2

I have two crayons.

A
B
C
D
E
F
G
H
I
J
K
L
M
N
O
P
Q
R
S
(T)
U
V
W
X
Y
Z

119

Ss Tt Activity Page

Word List

sandwich	shirt	skunk	sky	snake
spider	tail	tent	tree	turtle

Read each word in the Word List. Then point to the object that goes with each word in the picture above.

Uu

ugly

That is an ugly fish!

umbrella

We stay cool under the umbrella.

uncle

My uncle is my dad's brother.

under

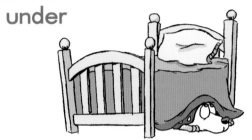

Blue is under the bed.

up

My kite is up in the air.

us

The blanket keeps us warm.

use

I use the computer at school.

121

Vv

vacation

Dad took us camping on our vacation.

valley

The house sits in a valley.

van

I take a ride in the van.

vegetable

What is your favorite vegetable?

very

Mouse is small. The bug is very small.

visit

I like to visit Grandma and Grandpa!

Ww

wait

Tiger and Gator wait for the bus.

wake

Don't wake Blue!

walk

I walk with Little Sister.

wall

My picture is on the wall.

want

I want a snack!

warm

My winter coat keeps me warm.

123

a
b
c
d
e
f
g
h
i
j
k
l
m
n
o
p
q
r
s
t
u
v
(w)
x
y
z

was

I was a cute baby.

wash, washes

We help wash the car.

watch, watches

We watch the baseball game.

watch, watches

Little Critter wears a watch.

water

Grandma and I play in the water.

wave

I wave to Maurice and Molly.

way

We know the way through the woods.

we

We play in the leaves.

wear

We wear our favorite pajamas.

week

There are seven days in a week.

wet

Our tent gets wet in the rain.

wheel

My bicycle has two wheels.

white

The polar bear has white fur.

a
b
c
d
e
f
g
h
i
j
k
l
m
n
o
p
q
r
s
t
u
v
w
x
y
z

win

We win the race.

windy

It is windy in the spring.

window

Little Sister looks out the window.

winter

It snows in the winter.

wish, wishes

Little Sister makes a wish.

woman, women

The woman has brown hair.

wood

I build a doghouse out of wood.

word

That is a long word.

work

I work in the garden with Grandma.

world

The rocket flies around the world.

worm

Yuck! There is a worm in my apple!

write

I write a letter to Grandma and Grandpa.

A
B
C
D
E
F
G
H
I
J
K
L
M
N
O
P
Q
R
S
T
U
V
W
X
Y
Z

Uu Vv Ww Activity Page

Word List

umbrella	under	van	vegetables
white	window	woman	worm

Read each word in the Word List. Then point to the object that goes with each word.

128

Xx - Yy

A
B
C
D
E
F
G
H
I
J
K
L
M
N
O
P
Q
R
S
T
U
V
W
X
Y
Z

x-ray

The doctor looks at an x-ray of my bones.

xylophone

I can play the xylophone.

yard

There is a fence around the yard.

yarn

Kitty plays with a ball of yarn.

year

spring   summer   fall   winter

There are four seasons in a year.

yell

I yell at Bun Bun.

yellow

The banana is yellow.

129

a
b
c
d
e
f
g
h
i
j
k
l
m
n
o
p
q
r
s
t
u
v
w
x
y
z

Yy-Zz

yes

Yes, I would like a hot dog.

you

You are my friend!

your

My ball is yellow. Your ball is red.

zebra

A zebra has black and white stripes.

zip

I zip my coat.

zipper

Pull the zipper down to open it.

zoo

Many animals live at the zoo.

Xx Yy Zz Activity Page

Read each word in the Word List. Then point to the object that goes with each word.

At School

Read each word in the Word List. Then point to the object that goes with each word in the picture above.

Color Words

Word List

black   blue   brown   green   orange
purple   red   white   yellow

Point to one food item that is the color of each word in the Word List.

Parts of the Body

Point to the parts of the body in the Word List that you see on Little Critter or Mouse. Then point to the same ones on you.

134

At Home

Word List

bag	banana	bowl	bread	fork
glass	grapes	oven	pie	plate
refrigerator	spoon	table	telephone	vegetables

Read each word in the Word List. Then point to the object that goes with each word in the picture above.

Find the Toys

Read each word in the Word List. Then point to the object that goes with each word in the picture above.

Number Words

one two three four five six seven eight nine ten

Point to the critter who has **one** thing. Then point to the critter who has **two** things.
Repeat for the numbers **three, four, five, six, seven, eight, nine,** and **ten.**

Aa Bb Activity Page

Word List

airplane	alligator	ant	ball
baseball	bear	blocks	

Read each word in the Word List. Then point to the object that goes with each word in the picture above.

26

Cc Dd Activity Page

Word List

cake	cat	chair	cookie
dish	doll	dress	duck

Read each word in the Word List. Then point to the object that goes with each word in the picture above.

39

Ee Ff Activity Page

Word List

ear	egg	eight	elephant
fish	flower	fox	frog

Read each word in the Word List. Then point to the object that goes with each word.

49

Gg Hh Activity Page

goldfish	hug
goose	hat
house	goose
hug	goat
game	goldfish
goat	heart
hat	game
heart	house

Look at each picture in the column on the left. Then point to the word that matches the picture in the column on the right.

61

138

Ii Jj Activity Page

Word List

ice	ice cream	jam
jar	jeans	juice

Read each word in the Word List. Then point to the object that goes with each word in the picture above.

65

Kk Ll Activity Page

Word List

key	king	kite	kitten
lamp	lemonade	lion	log

Read each word in the Word List. Then point to the object that goes with each word.

74

Mm Nn Activity Page

Word List

milk	mittens	monkey	mouse
nest	nine	nurse	nut

Read each word in the Word List. Then point to the object that goes with each word.

82

Oo Pp Activity Page

Word List

octopus	open	orange	owl
pail	pencil	pig	pumpkin

Read each word in the Word List. Then point to the object that goes with each word.

93

Qq Rr Activity Page

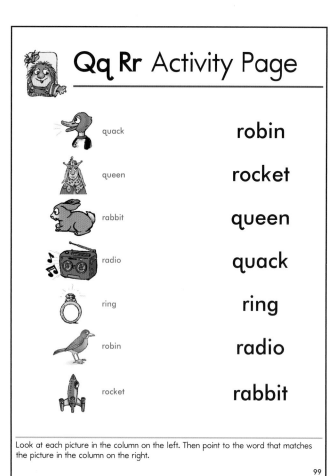

quack   robin

queen   rocket

rabbit   queen

radio   quack

ring   ring

robin   radio

rocket   rabbit

Look at each picture in the column on the left. Then point to the word that matches the picture in the column on the right.

99

Ss Tt Activity Page

Word List

sandwich	shirt	skunk	sky	snake
spider	tail	tent	tree	turtle

Read each word in the Word List. Then point to the object that goes with each word in the picture above.

120

Uu Vv Ww Activity Page

Word List

umbrella	under	van	vegetables
white	window	woman	worm

Read each word in the Word List. Then point to the object that goes with each word.

128

Xx Yy Zz Activity Page

Word List

x-ray	xylophone	yarn
zebra	zipper	zoo

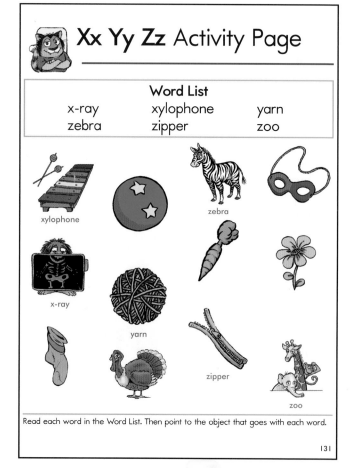

Read each word in the Word List. Then point to the object that goes with each word.

131

At School

Word List

alphabet	book	chair	clock	computer
crayons	desk	flag	paper	pen
pencil	sticker	teacher	window	

Read each word in the Word List. Then point to the object that goes with each word in the picture above.

132

Color Words

Word List

black	blue	brown	green	orange
purple	red	white	yellow	

Point to one food item that is the color of each word in the Word List.

133

Parts of the Body

Word List

arm
ear
elbow
eye
face
finger
foot
hair
hand
head
knee
leg
mouth
nose
toe
tooth
tummy

Point to the parts of the body in the Word List that you see on Little Critter or Mouse. Then point to the same ones on you.

134

At Home

Word List

bag	banana	bowl	bread	fork
glass	grapes	oven	pie	plate
refrigerator	spoon	table	telephone	vegetables

Read each word in the Word List. Then point to the object that goes with each word in the picture above.

135

141

Find the Toys

Word List

ball	car	dinosaur
robot	skateboard	skates
tractor	train	tricycle

Read each word in the Word List. Then point to the object that goes with each word in the picture above.

136

Number Words

4-four

7-seven

5-five

2-two

6-six

8-eight

1-one

10-ten

3-three

9-nine

1	2	3	4	5	6	7	8	9	10
one	two	three	four	five	six	seven	eight	nine	ten

Point to the Critter who has **one** thing. Then point to the Critter who has **two** things. Repeat for the numbers **three, four, five, six, seven, eight, nine,** and **ten.**

137